HAL•LEONARD

JAZZ PLAY-ALONG®

Book and CD for B♭, E♭, C and Bass Clef Instruments

2nd Edition

JAZZ IN THREE

Arranged and Produced by Mark Taylor

volume 31

T0055445

BOOK

TITLE	PAGE NUMBERS			
	C Treble Instruments	B♭ Instruments	E♭ Instruments	C Bass Instruments
Alice in Wonderland	4	20	36	52
Bluesette	6	22	38	54
Gravy Waltz	8	24	40	56
Jitterbug Waltz	10	26	42	58
Moon River	12	28	44	60
Oh, What a Beautiful Mornin'	14	30	46	62
Tenderly	9	25	41	57
West Coast Blues	16	32	48	64
What'll I Do?	17	33	49	65
Wives and Lovers (Hey, Little Girl)	18	34	50	66

CD

TITLE	CD Track Number Split Track / Melody	CD Track Number Full Stereo Track
Alice in Wonderland	1	2
Bluesette	3	4
Gravy Waltz	5	6
Jitterbug Waltz	7	8
Moon River	9	10
Oh, What a Beautiful Mornin'	11	12
Tenderly	13	14
West Coast Blues	15	16
What'll I Do?	17	18
Wives and Lovers (Hey, Little Girl)	19	20
B♭ Tuning Notes		21

ISBN 978-0-634-06856-0

HAL•LEONARD® CORPORATION

7777 W. Bluemound Rd. P.O. Box 13819 Milwaukee, WI 53213

For all works contained herein:
Unauthorized copying, arranging, adapting, recording or public performance is an infringement of copyright.
Infringers are liable under the law.

Visit Hal Leonard Online at
www.halleonard.com

Jazz in Three

Volume 31

Arranged and Produced by
Mark Taylor

Featured Players:

Graham Breedlove–Trumpet
John Desalme–Tenor Sax
Tony Nalker–Piano
Jim Roberts–Bass
Steve Fidyk–Drums

Recorded at Bias Studios, Springfield, Virginia
Bob Dawson, Engineer

HOW TO USE THE CD:

Each song has two tracks:

1) Split Track/Melody

Woodwind, Brass, Keyboard, and **Mallet Players** can use this track as a learning tool for melody style and inflection.

Bass Players can learn and perform with this track – remove the recorded bass track by turning down the volume on the LEFT channel.

Keyboard and **Guitar Players** can learn and perform with this track – remove the recorded piano part by turning down the volume on the RIGHT channel.

2) Full Stereo Track

Soloists or **Groups** can learn and perform with this accompaniment track with the RHYTHM SECTION only.

CD

1 : SPLIT TRACK/MELODY

2 : FULL STEREO TRACK

ALICE IN WONDERLAND

FROM WALT DISNEY'S ALICE IN WONDERLAND

C VERSION

WORDS BY BOB HILLIARD
MUSIC BY SAMMY FAIN

© 1951 Walt Disney Music Company
Copyright Renewed
This arrangement © 2002 Walt Disney Music Company
All Rights Reserved Used by Permission

SOLOS
Dmi7 G7 CMA7 FMA7 Bmi7(b5) E7 Ami7 Eb7
Dmi7 G7 Emi7 Ami7 Dmi7 G7 1. Emi7 A7(b9)
2. CMA7 A+7(#9) D7 G7 Emi7 Ami7 Dmi7 G7
CMA7 FMA7 F#mi7(b5) B+7(b9) Emi7 A7
Dmi7 A+7 Dmi7 G7 Dmi7 G7 CMA7 FMA7
Bmi7(b5) E7 Ami7 Eb7 Dmi7 G7
D.C. AL CODA
Emi7 Ami7 Dmi7 G7 C6/9 Eb13(#11)
CODA
C6/9 BbMA9 AbMA9 G7SUS CMA13(#11)
RIT.

CD

3 : SPLIT TRACK/MELODY

4 : FULL STEREO TRACK

BLUESETTE

WORDS BY NORMAN GIMBEL
MUSIC BY JEAN THIELEMANS

C VERSION

Copyright © 1963, 1964 SONGS OF UNIVERSAL, INC.
Copyright Renewed; Words Renewed 1992 by NORMAN GIMBEL for the World and Assigned to NEW THUNDER MUSIC, INC.
Administered by GIMBEL MUSIC GROUP, INC. (P.O. Box 15221, Beverly Hills, CA 90209 USA)
This arrangement Copyright © 2005 by NORMAN GIMBEL for the World
and Assigned to NEW THUNDER MUSIC, INC. Administered by GIMBEL MUSIC GROUP, INC. (P.O. Box 15221, Beverly Hills, CA 90209 USA)
All Rights Reserved Used by Permission

Fmi7
Bb7(b9)
EbMA7
Ebmi7
Ab9

DbMA7
Dbmi7
Gb9
CbMA7

Cmi7(b5)
F13
F/Eb
Dmi7
Db7
Cmi7
F7

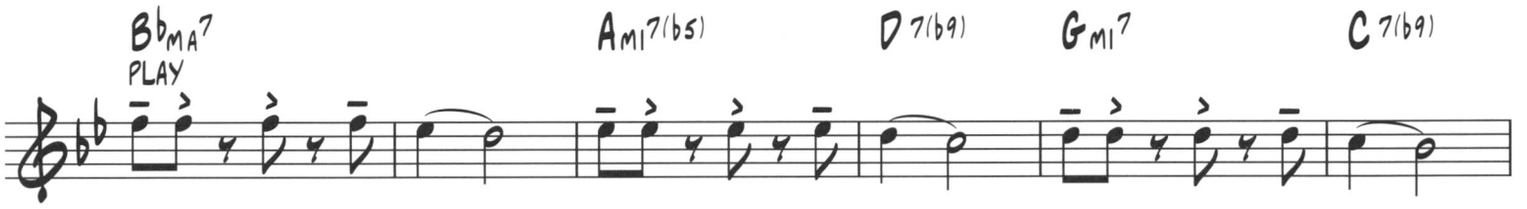
BbMA7
PLAY
Ami7(b5)
D7(b9)
Gmi7
C7(b9)

Fmi7
Bb7(b9)
EbMA7
Ebmi7
Ab9

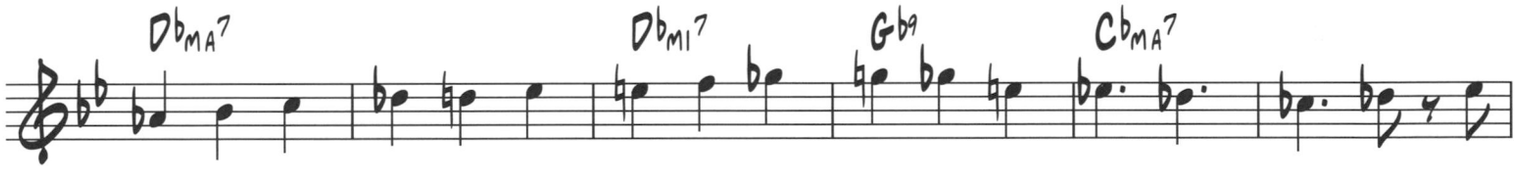
DbMA7
Dbmi7
Gb9
CbMA7

D.S. AL CODA
Cmi7(b5)
F13
F/Eb
Dmi7
Db7
Cmi7
F7

CODA
Dmi11
G7
Cmi11

F13
BbMA9
F9SUS
PLAY 4 TIMES
BbMA9

CD

5 : SPLIT TRACK/MELODY
6 : FULL STEREO TRACK

GRAVY WALTZ

LYRICS BY STEVE ALLEN
MUSIC BY RAY BROWN

C VERSION

© 1962, 1963 (Renewed 1990, 1991) SCREEN GEMS-EMI MUSIC INC.
This arrangement © 2005 SCREEN GEMS-EMI MUSIC INC.
All Rights Reserved International Copyright Secured Used by Permission

CD

13 : SPLIT TRACK/MELODY

14 : FULL STEREO TRACK

C VERSION

TENDERLY

FROM TORCH SONG

LYRIC BY JACK LAWRENCE
MUSIC BY WALTER GROSS

© 1946, 1947 EDWIN H. MORRIS & COMPANY, A Division of MPL Music Publishing, Inc.
Copyright Renewed, extended term of Copyright deriving from Jack Lawrence assigned and effective August 7, 2002 to RANGE ROAD MUSIC INC.
This arrangement © 2005 EDWIN H. MORRIS & COMPANY, A Division of MPL Music Publishing, Inc. and RANGE ROAD MUSIC INC.
All Rights Reserved

CD

7 : SPLIT TRACK/MELODY

8 : FULL STEREO TRACK

JITTERBUG WALTZ

MUSIC BY THOMAS "FATS" WALLER

C VERSION

Copyright © 1942 by Chappell & Co.
Copyright Renewed
This arrangement Copyright © 2005 by Chappell & Co.
International Copyright Secured All Rights Reserved

SOLO
Eb6/9
Ab9
Eb6/9
Gmi7
C7
Gmi7
C7
F9
Abmi7
Db9(#11)
F9
Bb9
1.
Gmi7
C7(b9)
D.S. AL CODA
TAKE 1ST ENDING
Fmi7
Bb7(b9)
2.
Eb6/9
Gb13
Fmi7
Bb13
CODA
Eb6/9
Ab9
Eb6/9
Eb6
E9
Eb6

CD

9 : SPLIT TRACK/MELODY

10 : FULL STEREO TRACK

MOON RIVER

FROM THE PARAMOUNT PICTURE BREAKFAST AT TIFFANY'S

WORDS BY JOHNNY MERCER
MUSIC BY HENRY MANCINI

C VERSION

Copyright © 1961 Sony/ATV Music Publishing LLC
Copyright Renewed
This arrangement Copyright © 2005 Sony/ATV Music Publishing LLC
All Rights Administered by Sony/ATV Music Publishing LLC, 8 Music Square West, Nashville, TN 37203
International Copyright Secured All Rights Reserved

TO CODA
CMA9
AMI7
Ab13(#11)
G9SUS
G13(b9)
CMA9
BbMA9
SOLO BREAK
CMA9
BbMA9
CMA9
BbMA9
G13SUS
G+7(#9)
SOLOS (2 FULL CHORUSES)
CMA9
AMI7
FMA13(#11)
CMA9
FMA13(#11)
CMA9
BMI7(b5)
E7(b9)
1.
AMI7
C7/G
FMA9
Bb9(#11)
AMI7
AMI7/G
F#MI7(b5)
B9
EMI7
A9
DMI7
G9
2.
AMI7
AMI7/G
F#MI7(b5)
F13(#11)
CMA9
FMA9
CMA9
FMA9
CMA9
AMI7
Ab13(#11)
G9SUS
CMA9
G9SUS
D.S. AL CODA
CODA
CMA9
BbMA9
CMA9
BbMA9
RHYTHM
CMA9
BbMA9
CMA9
PLAY
BbMA9
AbMA9
G+7(#9)
CMA13(#11)
mf

CD

11 : SPLIT TRACK/MELODY

12 : FULL STEREO TRACK

C VERSION

OH, WHAT A BEAUTIFUL MORNIN'

FROM OKLAHOMA!

LYRICS BY OSCAR HAMMERSTEIN II
MUSIC BY RICHARD RODGERS

Copyright © 1943 by WILLIAMSON MUSIC
Copyright Renewed
This arrangement Copyright © 2005 by WILLIAMSON MUSIC
International Copyright Secured All Rights Reserved

SOLOS (3 CHORUSES)
E♭MA7 F MI7/E♭ E♭MA9 F MI7/E♭ E♭MA7 F MI7/E♭
E♭MA9 D♭9(♯11) E♭MA7 F MI7 G MI7 A♭MA7
G MI7 C7(♯11)(♭9) F MI7 B♭13(♭9) E♭MA9
A13 A♭6/9 G MI7 C MI9 F13 F+7 B♭9SUS B♭13(♭9)
E♭MA9 A7(♭5) A♭13(♯11) A°7 E♭6/B♭ B♭9
D.S. AL CODA
LAST TIME
E♭MA7 F MI7/E♭ E♭MA9 B♭9SUS B♭13(♭9)
CODA
B♭13SUS B♭9 G+7(♯9) C9 F MI9 B♭9
E♭MA7 F MI7/E♭ E♭MA9 F MI7/E♭ E♭MA7
PLAY 3 TIMES

CD

15 : SPLIT TRACK/MELODY

16 : FULL STEREO TRACK

WEST COAST BLUES

BY JOHN L. (WES) MONTGOMERY

C VERSION

Copyright © 1960 (Renewed) by TAGGIE MUSIC CO., a division of Gopam Enterprises, Inc.
This arrangement Copyright © 2005 by TAGGIE MUSIC CO., a division of Gopam Enterprises, Inc.
All Rights Reserved Used by Permission

CD

17: SPLIT TRACK/MELODY

18: FULL STEREO TRACK

C VERSION

WHAT'LL I DO?

FROM MUSIC BOX REVUE OF 1924

WORDS AND MUSIC BY
IRVING BERLIN

© Copyright 1924 by Irving Berlin
© Arrangement Copyright 1947 by Irving Berlin
Copyright Renewed
This arrangement © Copyright 2002 by the Estate of Irving Berlin
International Copyright Secured All Rights Reserved

CD

19 : SPLIT TRACK/MELODY

20 : FULL STEREO TRACK

C VERSION

WIVES AND LOVERS

(HEY, LITTLE GIRL)

FROM THE PARAMOUNT PICTURE WIVES AND LOVERS

WORDS BY HAL DAVID
MUSIC BY BURT BACHARACH

Copyright © 1963 Sony/ATV Music Publishing LLC
Copyright Renewed
This arrangement Copyright © 2005 Sony/ATV Music Publishing LLC
All Rights Administered by Sony/ATV Music Publishing LLC, 8 Music Square West, Nashville, TN 37203
International Copyright Secured All Rights Reserved

SOLOS (2 CHORUSES)
Bb13sus
Bb9sus
Bb9
C13sus
C9sus
C9
Cmi9
F13(b9)
Ami7(b5)
D9sus
D+7(#9)
EbMA9
Ami11
Ab13(#11)
D7(b9)
DbMA9
C13sus
Bb13sus
PLAY
mf
1.
Bb9sus
2.
Bb9sus
Db9(#11)
C9sus
Bb9sus
AbMA9
Gb13sus
Fmi11
E13sus
EbMA13(#11)
MOLTO RIT.

CD

1 : SPLIT TRACK/MELODY

2 : FULL STEREO TRACK

ALICE IN WONDERLAND

FROM WALT DISNEY'S ALICE IN WONDERLAND

© 1951 Walt Disney Music Company
Copyright Renewed
This arrangement © 2002 Walt Disney Music Company
All Rights Reserved Used by Permission

SOLOS
EMI7 A7 DMA7 GMA7 C#MI7(b5) F#7 BMI7 F7
EMI7 A7 F#MI7 BMI7 EMI7 A7 1. F#MI7 B7(b9)
2. DMA7 B+7(#9) E7 A7 F#MI7 BMI7 EMI7 A7
DMA7 GMA7 G#MI7(b5) C#+7(b9) F#MI7 B7
EMI7 B+7 EMI7 A7 EMI7 A7 DMA7 GMA7
C#MI7(b5) F#7 BMI7 F7 EMI7 A7
D.C. AL CODA
F#MI7 BMI7 EMI7 A7 D6/9 F13(#11)
CODA
D6/9 CMA9 BbMA9 A7SUS DMA13(#11)
RIT.

CD

3 : SPLIT TRACK/MELODY

4 : FULL STEREO TRACK

BLUESETTE

WORDS BY NORMAN GIMBEL
MUSIC BY JEAN THIELEMANS

Copyright © 1963, 1964 SONGS OF UNIVERSAL, INC.
Copyright Renewed; Words Renewed 1992 by NORMAN GIMBEL for the World and Assigned to NEW THUNDER MUSIC, INC.
Administered by GIMBEL MUSIC GROUP, INC. (P.O. Box 15221, Beverly Hills, CA 90209 USA)
This arrangement Copyright © 2005 by NORMAN GIMBEL for the World
and Assigned to NEW THUNDER MUSIC, INC. Administered by GIMBEL MUSIC GROUP, INC. (P.O. Box 15221, Beverly Hills, CA 90209 USA)
All Rights Reserved Used by Permission

Gmi7
C7(b9)
FMA7
Fmi7
Bb9
EbMA7
Ebmi7
Ab9
DbMA7
Dmi7(b5)
G13
G/F
Emi7
Eb7
Dmi7
G7
CMA7
PLAY
Bmi7(b5)
E7(b9)
Ami7
D7(b9)
Gmi7
C7(b9)
FMA7
Fmi7
Bb9
EbMA7
Ebmi7
Ab9
DbMA7
D.S. AL CODA
Dmi7(b5)
G13
G/F
Emi7
Eb7
Dmi7
G7
CODA
Emi11
A7
Dmi11
G13
CMA9
G9SUS
PLAY 4 TIMES
CMA9

CD

5 : SPLIT TRACK/MELODY

6 : FULL STEREO TRACK

GRAVY WALTZ

LYRICS BY STEVE ALLEN
MUSIC BY RAY BROWN

© 1962, 1963 (Renewed 1990, 1991) SCREEN GEMS-EMI MUSIC INC.
This arrangement © 2005 SCREEN GEMS-EMI MUSIC INC.
All Rights Reserved International Copyright Secured Used by Permission

CD

13 : SPLIT TRACK/MELODY

14 : FULL STEREO TRACK

TENDERLY

FROM TORCH SONG

LYRIC BY JACK LAWRENCE
MUSIC BY WALTER GROSS

B♭ VERSION

© 1946, 1947 EDWIN H. MORRIS & COMPANY, A Division of MPL Music Publishing, Inc.
Copyright Renewed, extended term of Copyright deriving from Jack Lawrence assigned and effective August 7, 2002 to RANGE ROAD MUSIC INC.
This arrangement © 2005 EDWIN H. MORRIS & COMPANY, A Division of MPL Music Publishing, Inc. and RANGE ROAD MUSIC INC.
All Rights Reserved

CD

7 : SPLIT TRACK/MELODY

8 : FULL STEREO TRACK

JITTERBUG WALTZ

MUSIC BY THOMAS "FATS" WALLER

Copyright © 1942 by Chappell & Co.
Copyright Renewed
This arrangement Copyright © 2005 by Chappell & Co.
International Copyright Secured All Rights Reserved

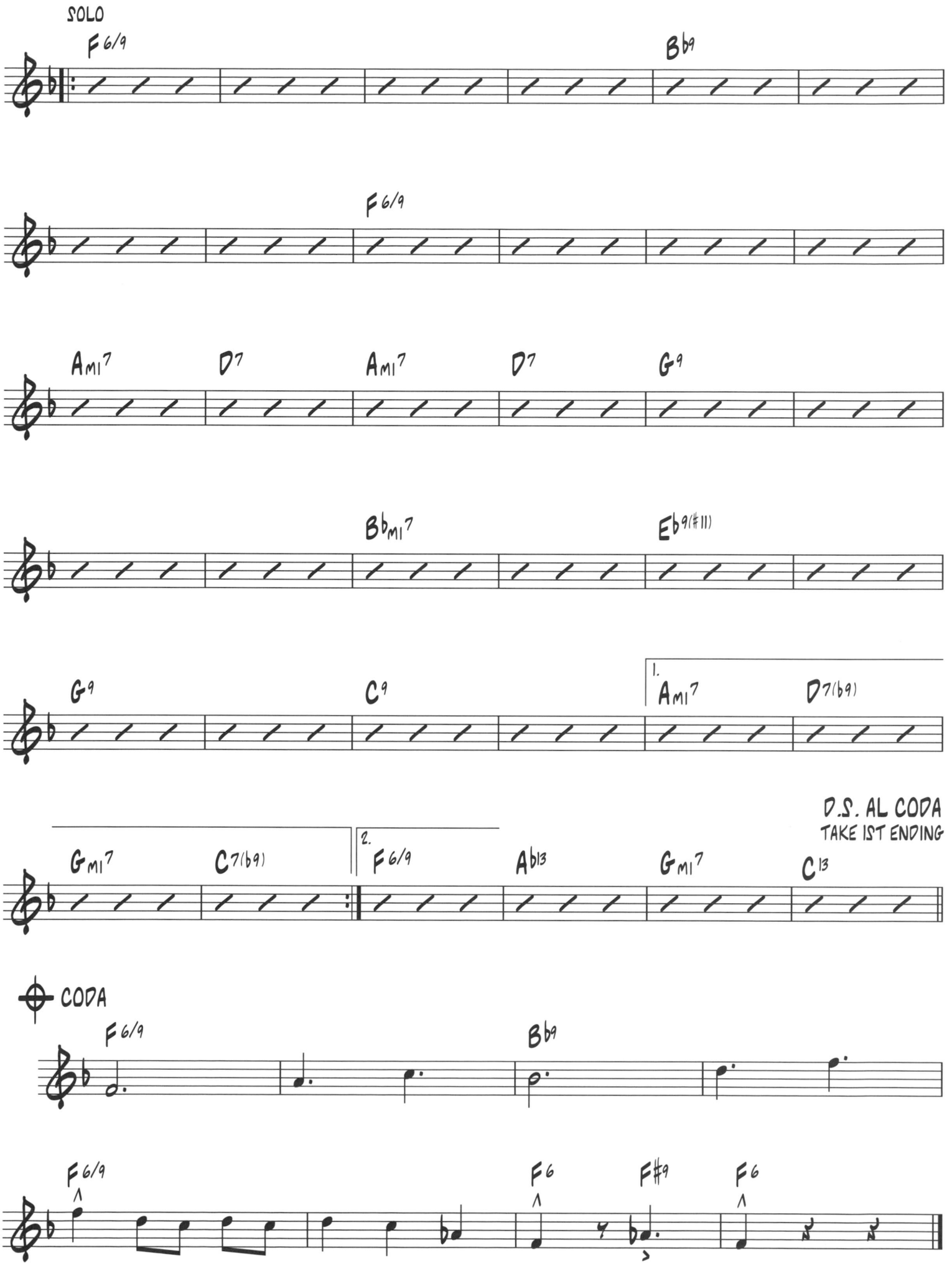
SOLO
F6/9
Bb9
F6/9
Ami7
D7
Ami7
D7
G9
Bbmi7
Eb9(#11)
G9
C9
1.
Ami7
D7(b9)
D.S. AL CODA
TAKE 1ST ENDING
Gmi7
C7(b9)
2.
F6/9
Ab13
Gmi7
C13
CODA
F6/9
Bb9
F6/9
F6
F#9
F6

CD

9 : SPLIT TRACK/MELODY

10 : FULL STEREO TRACK

MOON RIVER

FROM THE PARAMOUNT PICTURE BREAKFAST AT TIFFANY'S

WORDS BY JOHNNY MERCER
MUSIC BY HENRY MANCINI

B♭ VERSION

Copyright © 1961 Sony/ATV Music Publishing LLC
Copyright Renewed
This arrangement Copyright © 2005 Sony/ATV Music Publishing LLC
All Rights Administered by Sony/ATV Music Publishing LLC, 8 Music Square West, Nashville, TN 37203
International Copyright Secured All Rights Reserved

TO CODA
DMA9
BMI7
Bb13(#11)
A9SUS
A13(b9)
DMA9
CMA9
SOLO BREAK
DMA9
CMA9
DMA9
CMA9
A13SUS
A+7(#9)
SOLOS (2 FULL CHORUSES)
DMA9
BMI7
GMA13(#11)
DMA9
GMA13(#11)
DMA9
C#MI7(b5)
F#7(b9)
1.
BMI7
D7/A
GMA9
C9(#11)
BMI7
BMI7/A
G#MI7(b5)
C#9
F#MI7
B9
EMI7
A9
2.
BMI7
BMI7/A
G#MI7(b5)
G13(#11)
DMA9
GMA9
DMA9
GMA9
DMA9
D.S. AL CODA
BMI7
Bb13(#11)
A9SUS
DMA9
A9SUS
CODA
DMA9
CMA9
DMA9
CMA9
RHYTHM
DMA9
CMA9
DMA9
PLAY
CMA9
BbMA9
A+7(#9)
DMA13(#11)
mf

CD

11 : SPLIT TRACK/MELODY
12 : FULL STEREO TRACK

OH, WHAT A BEAUTIFUL MORNIN'

FROM OKLAHOMA!

LYRICS BY OSCAR HAMMERSTEIN II
MUSIC BY RICHARD RODGERS

B♭ VERSION

Copyright © 1943 by WILLIAMSON MUSIC
Copyright Renewed
This arrangement Copyright © 2005 by WILLIAMSON MUSIC
International Copyright Secured All Rights Reserved

SOLOS (3 CHORUSES)
FMA7 GMI7/F FMA9 GMI7/F FMA7 GMI7/F
FMA9 Eb9(#11) FMA7 GMI7 AMI7 BbMA7
AMI7 D7(#11)(b9) GMI7 C13(b9) FMA9
B13 Bb6/9 AMI7 DMI9 G13 G+7 C9SUS C13(b9)
FMA9 B7(b5) Bb13(#11) B07 F6/C C9
D.S. AL CODA
LAST TIME
FMA7 GMI7/F FMA9 C9SUS C13(b9)
CODA
C13SUS C9 A+7(#9) D9 GMI9 C9
FMA7 GMI7/F FMA9 GMI7/F FMA7
PLAY 3 TIMES

CD

15 : SPLIT TRACK/MELODY

16 : FULL STEREO TRACK

WEST COAST BLUES

BY JOHN L. (WES) MONTGOMERY

B♭ VERSION

Copyright © 1960 (Renewed) by TAGGIE MUSIC CO., a division of Gopam Enterprises, Inc.
This arrangement Copyright © 2005 by TAGGIE MUSIC CO., a division of Gopam Enterprises, Inc.
All Rights Reserved Used by Permission

CD

17 : SPLIT TRACK/MELODY

18 : FULL STEREO TRACK

B♭ VERSION

WHAT'LL I DO?

FROM MUSIC BOX REVUE OF 1924

WORDS AND MUSIC BY
IRVING BERLIN

© Copyright 1924 by Irving Berlin
© Arrangement Copyright 1947 by Irving Berlin
Copyright Renewed
This arrangement © Copyright 2002 by the Estate of Irving Berlin
International Copyright Secured All Rights Reserved

CD

19 : SPLIT TRACK/MELODY

20 : FULL STEREO TRACK

B♭ VERSION

WIVES AND LOVERS

(HEY, LITTLE GIRL)

FROM THE PARAMOUNT PICTURE WIVES AND LOVERS

WORDS BY HAL DAVID
MUSIC BY BURT BACHARACH

Copyright © 1963 Sony/ATV Music Publishing LLC
Copyright Renewed
This arrangement Copyright © 2005 Sony/ATV Music Publishing LLC
All Rights Administered by Sony/ATV Music Publishing LLC, 8 Music Square West, Nashville, TN 37203
International Copyright Secured All Rights Reserved

SOLOS (2 CHORUSES)
C13SUS
C9SUS
C9
D13SUS
D9SUS
D9
DMI9
G13(b9)
BMI7(b5)
E9SUS
E+7(#9)
FMA9
BMI11
Bb13(#11)
E7(b9)
EbMA9
D13SUS
C13SUS
PLAY
mf
1.
C9SUS
2.
C9SUS
Eb9(#11)
D9SUS
C9SUS
BbMA9
Ab13SUS
GMI11
F#13SUS
FMA13(#11)
MOLTO RIT.

CD

1 : SPLIT TRACK/MELODY
2 : FULL STEREO TRACK

ALICE IN WONDERLAND

FROM WALT DISNEY'S ALICE IN WONDERLAND

E♭ VERSION

WORDS BY BOB HILLIARD
MUSIC BY SAMMY FAIN

© 1951 Walt Disney Music Company
Copyright Renewed
This arrangement © 2002 Walt Disney Music Company
All Rights Reserved Used by Permission

SOLOS
Bmi7 E7 AMA7 DMA7 G#mi7(b5) C#7 F#mi7 C7
Bmi7 E7 C#mi7 F#mi7 Bmi7 E7 1. C#mi7 F#7(b9)
2. AMA7 F#+7(#9) B7 E7 C#mi7 F#mi7 Bmi7 E7
AMA7 DMA7 D#mi7(b5) G#+7(b9) C#mi7 F#7
Bmi7 F#+7 Bmi7 E7 Bmi7 E7 AMA7 DMA7
G#mi7(b5) C#7 F#mi7 C7 Bmi7 E7
D.C. AL CODA
C#mi7 F#mi7 Bmi7 E7 A6/9 C13(#11)
CODA
A6/9 GMA9 FMA9 E7SUS AMA13(#11)
RIT.

CD

3 : SPLIT TRACK/MELODY

4 : FULL STEREO TRACK

BLUESETTE

WORDS BY NORMAN GIMBEL
MUSIC BY JEAN THIELEMANS

Copyright © 1963, 1964 SONGS OF UNIVERSAL, INC.
Copyright Renewed; Words Renewed 1992 by NORMAN GIMBEL for the World and Assigned to NEW THUNDER MUSIC, INC.
Administered by GIMBEL MUSIC GROUP, INC. (P.O. Box 15221, Beverly Hills, CA 90209 USA)
This arrangement Copyright © 2005 by NORMAN GIMBEL for the World
and Assigned to NEW THUNDER MUSIC, INC. Administered by GIMBEL MUSIC GROUP, INC. (P.O. Box 15221, Beverly Hills, CA 90209 USA)
All Rights Reserved Used by Permission

Dmi7
G7(b9)
CMA7
Cmi7
F9
BbMA7
Bbmi7
Eb9
AbMA7
Ami7(b5)
D13
D/C
Bmi7
Bb7
Ami7
D7
GMA7
PLAY
F#mi7(b5)
B7(b9)
Emi7
A7(b9)
Dmi7
G7(b9)
CMA7
Cmi7
F9
BbMA7
Bbmi7
Eb9
AbMA7
Ami7(b5)
D13
D/C
Bmi7
Bb7
Ami7
D7
D.S. AL CODA
CODA
Bmi11
E7
Ami11
D13
GMA9
D9SUS
PLAY 4 TIMES
GMA9

CD

5 : SPLIT TRACK/MELODY

6 : FULL STEREO TRACK

GRAVY WALTZ

LYRICS BY STEVE ALLEN
MUSIC BY RAY BROWN

© 1962, 1963 (Renewed 1990, 1991) SCREEN GEMS-EMI MUSIC INC.
This arrangement © 2005 SCREEN GEMS-EMI MUSIC INC.
All Rights Reserved International Copyright Secured Used by Permission

CD

13 : SPLIT TRACK/MELODY

14 : FULL STEREO TRACK

TENDERLY

FROM TORCH SONG

LYRIC BY JACK LAWRENCE
MUSIC BY WALTER GROSS

© 1946, 1947 EDWIN H. MORRIS & COMPANY, A Division of MPL Music Publishing, Inc.
Copyright Renewed, extended term of Copyright deriving from Jack Lawrence assigned and effective August 7, 2002 to RANGE ROAD MUSIC INC.
This arrangement © 2005 EDWIN H. MORRIS & COMPANY, A Division of MPL Music Publishing, Inc. and RANGE ROAD MUSIC INC.
All Rights Reserved

CD

7 : SPLIT TRACK/MELODY

8 : FULL STEREO TRACK

JITTERBUG WALTZ

MUSIC BY THOMAS "FATS" WALLER

Copyright © 1942 by Chappell & Co.
Copyright Renewed
This arrangement Copyright © 2005 by Chappell & Co.
International Copyright Secured All Rights Reserved

SOLO
C6/9
F9
C6/9
Emi7
A7
Emi7
A7
D9
Fmi7
Bb9(#11)
D9
G9
1.
Emi7
A7(b9)
D.S. AL CODA
TAKE 1ST ENDING
Dmi7
G7(b9)
2.
C6/9
Eb13
Dmi7
G13
CODA
C6/9
F9
C6/9
C6
C#9
C6

CD

9 : SPLIT TRACK/MELODY

10 : FULL STEREO TRACK

MOON RIVER

FROM THE PARAMOUNT PICTURE BREAKFAST AT TIFFANY'S

WORDS BY JOHNNY MERCER
MUSIC BY HENRY MANCINI

E♭ VERSION

Copyright © 1961 Sony/ATV Music Publishing LLC
Copyright Renewed
This arrangement Copyright © 2005 Sony/ATV Music Publishing LLC
All Rights Administered by Sony/ATV Music Publishing LLC, 8 Music Square West, Nashville, TN 37203
International Copyright Secured All Rights Reserved

TO CODA
AMA9
F#MI7
F13(#11)
E9SUS
E13(b9)
AMA9
GMA9
SOLO BREAK
AMA9
GMA9
AMA9
GMA9
E13SUS
E+7(#9)
SOLOS (2 FULL CHORUSES)
AMA9
F#MI7
DMA13(#11)
AMA9
DMA13(#11)
AMA9
G#MI7(b5)
C#7(b9)
1.
F#MI7
A7/E
DMA9
G9(#11)
F#MI7
F#MI7/E
D#MI7(b5)
G#9
C#MI7
F#9
BMI7
E9
2.
F#MI7
F#MI7/E
D#MI7(b5)
D13(#11)
AMA9
DMA9
AMA9
DMA9
AMA9
D.S. AL CODA
F#MI7
F13(#11)
E9SUS
AMA9
E9SUS
CODA
AMA9
GMA9
AMA9
GMA9
RHYTHM
AMA9
GMA9
AMA9
PLAY
GMA9
FMA9
E+7(#9)
AMA13(#11)
mf

CD

11 : SPLIT TRACK/MELODY
12 : FULL STEREO TRACK

OH, WHAT A BEAUTIFUL MORNIN'

FROM OKLAHOMA!

LYRICS BY OSCAR HAMMERSTEIN II
MUSIC BY RICHARD RODGERS

E♭ VERSION

UP-TEMPO WALTZ

Copyright © 1943 by WILLIAMSON MUSIC
Copyright Renewed
This arrangement Copyright © 2005 by WILLIAMSON MUSIC
International Copyright Secured All Rights Reserved

SOLOS (3 CHORUSES)
CMA7
DMI7/C
CMA9
DMI7/C
CMA7
DMI7/C
CMA9
Bb9(#11)
CMA7
DMI7
EMI7
FMA7
EMI7
A7(#11)(b9)
DMI7
G13(b9)
CMA9
F#13
F6/9
EMI7
AMI9
D13
D+7
G9SUS
G13(b9)
CMA9
F#7(b5)
F13(#11)
F#07
C6/G
G9
D.S. AL CODA
LAST TIME
CMA7
DMI7/C
CMA9
G9SUS
G13(b9)
CODA
G13SUS
G9
E+7(#9)
A9
DMI9
G9
CMA7
DMI7/C
CMA9
DMI7/C
PLAY 3 TIMES
CMA7

CD

15 : SPLIT TRACK/MELODY

16 : FULL STEREO TRACK

WEST COAST BLUES

BY JOHN L. (WES) MONTGOMERY

Copyright © 1960 (Renewed) by TAGGIE MUSIC CO., a division of Gopam Enterprises, Inc.
This arrangement Copyright © 2005 by TAGGIE MUSIC CO., a division of Gopam Enterprises, Inc.
All Rights Reserved Used by Permission

CD

17 : SPLIT TRACK/MELODY

18 : FULL STEREO TRACK

WHAT'LL I DO?

FROM MUSIC BOX REVUE OF 1924

WORDS AND MUSIC BY
IRVING BERLIN

E♭ VERSION

© Copyright 1924 by Irving Berlin
© Arrangement Copyright 1947 by Irving Berlin
Copyright Renewed
This arrangement © Copyright 2002 by the Estate of Irving Berlin
International Copyright Secured All Rights Reserved

CD

19 : SPLIT TRACK/MELODY

20 : FULL STEREO TRACK

E♭ VERSION

WIVES AND LOVERS

(HEY, LITTLE GIRL)

FROM THE PARAMOUNT PICTURE WIVES AND LOVERS

WORDS BY HAL DAVID
MUSIC BY BURT BACHARACH

Copyright © 1963 Sony/ATV Music Publishing LLC
Copyright Renewed
This arrangement Copyright © 2005 Sony/ATV Music Publishing LLC
All Rights Administered by Sony/ATV Music Publishing LLC, 8 Music Square West, Nashville, TN 37203
International Copyright Secured All Rights Reserved

SOLOS (2 CHORUSES)
G13SUS
G9SUS
G9
A13SUS
A9SUS
A9
AMI9
D13(b9)
F#MI7(b5)
B9SUS
B+7(#9)
CMA9
F#MI11
F13(#11)
B7(b9)
BbMA9
A13SUS
G13SUS
PLAY
mf
1.
G9SUS
2.
G9SUS
Bb9(#11)
A9SUS
G9SUS
FMA9
Eb13SUS
DMI11
C#13SUS
CMA13(#11)
MOLTO RIT.

CD

: SPLIT TRACK/MELODY

: FULL STEREO TRACK

ALICE IN WONDERLAND

FROM WALT DISNEY'S ALICE IN WONDERLAND

© 1951 Walt Disney Music Company
Copyright Renewed
This arrangement © 2002 Walt Disney Music Company
All Rights Reserved Used by Permission

SOLOS
Dmi7 G7 CMA7 FMA7 Bmi7(b5) E7 Ami7 Eb7
Dmi7 G7 Emi7 Ami7 Dmi7 G7 1. Emi7 A7(b9)
2. CMA7 A+7(#9) D7 G7 Emi7 Ami7 Dmi7 G7
CMA7 FMA7 F#mi7(b5) B+7(b9) Emi7 A7
Dmi7 A+7 Dmi7 G7 Dmi7 G7 CMA7 FMA7
Bmi7(b5) E7 Ami7 Eb7 Dmi7 G7
D.C. AL CODA
Emi7 Ami7 Dmi7 G7 C6/9 Eb13(#11)
CODA
C6/9 BbMA9 AbMA9 G7SUS CMA13(#11)
RIT.

CD

3 : SPLIT TRACK/MELODY

: FULL STEREO TRACK

BLUESETTE

WORDS BY NORMAN GIMBEL
MUSIC BY JEAN THIELEMANS

Copyright © 1963, 1964 SONGS OF UNIVERSAL, INC.
Copyright Renewed; Words Renewed 1992 by NORMAN GIMBEL for the World and Assigned to NEW THUNDER MUSIC, INC.
Administered by GIMBEL MUSIC GROUP, INC. (P.O. Box 15221, Beverly Hills, CA 90209 USA)
This arrangement Copyright © 2005 by NORMAN GIMBEL for the World
and Assigned to NEW THUNDER MUSIC, INC. Administered by GIMBEL MUSIC GROUP, INC. (P.O. Box 15221, Beverly Hills, CA 90209 USA)
All Rights Reserved Used by Permission

Fmi7
Bb7(b9)
EbMA7
Ebmi7
Ab9
DbMA7
Dbmi7
Gb9
CbMA7
Cmi7(b5)
F13
F/Eb
Dmi7
Db7
Cmi7
F7
BbMA7
PLAY
Ami7(b5)
D7(b9)
Gmi7
C7(b9)
Fmi7
Bb7(b9)
EbMA7
Ebmi7
Ab9
DbMA7
Dbmi7
Gb9
CbMA7
Cmi7(b5)
F13
F/Eb
Dmi7
Db7
Cmi7
F7
D.S. AL CODA
CODA
Dmi11
G7
Cmi11
F13
BbMA9
F9SUS
PLAY 4 TIMES
BbMA9

CD

5 : SPLIT TRACK/MELODY

6 : FULL STEREO TRACK

GRAVY WALTZ

LYRICS BY STEVE ALLEN
MUSIC BY RAY BROWN

© 1962, 1963 (Renewed 1990, 1991) SCREEN GEMS-EMI MUSIC INC.
This arrangement © 2005 SCREEN GEMS-EMI MUSIC INC.
All Rights Reserved International Copyright Secured Used by Permission

CD

13 : SPLIT TRACK/MELODY

14 : FULL STEREO TRACK

TENDERLY

FROM TORCH SONG

LYRIC BY JACK LAWRENCE
MUSIC BY WALTER GROSS

© 1946, 1947 EDWIN H. MORRIS & COMPANY, A Division of MPL Music Publishing, Inc.
Copyright Renewed, extended term of Copyright deriving from Jack Lawrence assigned and effective August 7, 2002 to RANGE ROAD MUSIC INC.
This arrangement © 2005 EDWIN H. MORRIS & COMPANY, A Division of MPL Music Publishing, Inc. and RANGE ROAD MUSIC INC.
All Rights Reserved

CD

: SPLIT TRACK/MELODY

: FULL STEREO TRACK

JITTERBUG WALTZ

MUSIC BY THOMAS "FATS" WALLER

Copyright © 1942 by Chappell & Co.
Copyright Renewed
This arrangement Copyright © 2005 by Chappell & Co.
International Copyright Secured All Rights Reserved

SOLO
Eb6/9
Ab9
Eb6/9
Gmi7
C7
Gmi7
C7
F9
Abmi7
Db9(#11)
F9
Bb9
1.
Gmi7
C7(b9)
D.S. AL CODA
TAKE 1ST ENDING
Fmi7
Bb7(b9)
2.
Eb6/9
Gb13
Fmi7
Bb13
CODA
Eb6/9
Ab9
Eb6/9
Eb6
E9
Eb6

CD

9 : SPLIT TRACK/MELODY
10 : FULL STEREO TRACK

MOON RIVER

FROM THE PARAMOUNT PICTURE BREAKFAST AT TIFFANY'S

WORDS BY JOHNNY MERCER
MUSIC BY HENRY MANCINI

Copyright © 1961 Sony/ATV Music Publishing LLC
Copyright Renewed
This arrangement Copyright © 2005 Sony/ATV Music Publishing LLC
All Rights Administered by Sony/ATV Music Publishing LLC, 8 Music Square West, Nashville, TN 37203
International Copyright Secured All Rights Reserved

TO CODA
CMA9
AMI7
Ab13(#11)
G9SUS
G13(b9)
CMA9
BbMA9
SOLO BREAK
CMA9
BbMA9
CMA9
BbMA9
G13SUS
G+7(#9)
SOLOS (2 FULL CHORUSES)
CMA9
AMI7
FMA13(#11)
CMA9
FMA13(#11)
CMA9
BMI7(b5)
E7(b9)
1.
AMI7
C7/G
FMA9
Bb9(#11)
AMI7
AMI7/G
F#MI7(b5)
B9
EMI7
A9
DMI7
G9
2.
AMI7
AMI7/G
F#MI7(b5)
F13(#11)
CMA9
FMA9
CMA9
FMA9
CMA9
D.S. AL CODA
AMI7
Ab13(#11)
G9SUS
CMA9
G9SUS
CODA
CMA9
BbMA9
CMA9
BbMA9
RHYTHM
CMA9
BbMA9
CMA9
PLAY
BbMA9
AbMA9
G+7(#9)
CMA13(#11)
mf

CD

11 : SPLIT TRACK/MELODY

12 : FULL STEREO TRACK

OH, WHAT A BEAUTIFUL MORNIN'

FROM OKLAHOMA!

LYRICS BY OSCAR HAMMERSTEIN II
MUSIC BY RICHARD RODGERS

C VERSION

UP-TEMPO WALTZ

Copyright © 1943 by WILLIAMSON MUSIC
Copyright Renewed
This arrangement Copyright © 2005 by WILLIAMSON MUSIC
International Copyright Secured All Rights Reserved

SOLOS (3 CHORUSES)
Ebma7
Fmi7/Eb
Ebma9
Fmi7/Eb
Ebma7
Fmi7/Eb
Ebma9
Db9(#11)
Ebma7
Fmi7
Gmi7
Abma7
Gmi7
C7(#11)(b9)
Fmi7
Bb13(b9)
Ebma9
A13
Ab6/9
Gmi7
Cmi9
F13
F+7
Bb9sus
Bb13(b9)
Ebma9
A7(b5)
Ab13(#11)
A07
Eb6/Bb
Bb9
D.S. AL CODA
LAST TIME
Ebma7
Fmi7/Eb
Ebma9
Bb9sus
Bb13(b9)
CODA
Bb13sus
Bb9
G+7(#9)
C9
Fmi9
Bb9
Ebma7
Fmi7/Eb
Ebma9
Fmi7/Eb
PLAY 3 TIMES
Ebma7

CD

15 : SPLIT TRACK/MELODY

16 : FULL STEREO TRACK

WEST COAST BLUES

BY JOHN L. (WES) MONTGOMERY

Copyright © 1960 (Renewed) by TAGGIE MUSIC CO., a division of Gopam Enterprises, Inc.
This arrangement Copyright © 2005 by TAGGIE MUSIC CO., a division of Gopam Enterprises, Inc.
All Rights Reserved Used by Permission

CD

: SPLIT TRACK/MELODY

18: FULL STEREO TRACK

WHAT'LL I DO?

FROM MUSIC BOX REVUE OF 1924

WORDS AND MUSIC BY
IRVING BERLIN

© Copyright 1924 by Irving Berlin
© Arrangement Copyright 1947 by Irving Berlin
Copyright Renewed
This arrangement © Copyright 2002 by the Estate of Irving Berlin
International Copyright Secured All Rights Reserved

CD

19 : SPLIT TRACK/MELODY

20 : FULL STEREO TRACK

WIVES AND LOVERS

(HEY, LITTLE GIRL)

FROM THE PARAMOUNT PICTURE WIVES AND LOVERS

WORDS BY HAL DAVID
MUSIC BY BURT BACHARACH

Copyright © 1963 Sony/ATV Music Publishing LLC
Copyright Renewed
This arrangement Copyright © 2005 Sony/ATV Music Publishing LLC
All Rights Administered by Sony/ATV Music Publishing LLC, 8 Music Square West, Nashville, TN 37203
International Copyright Secured All Rights Reserved

SOLOS (2 CHORUSES)
Bb13sus
Bb9sus
Bb9
C13sus
C9sus
C9
Cmi9
F13(b9)
Ami7(b5)
D9sus
D+7(#9)
Ebma9
Ami11
Ab13(#11)
D7(b9)
Dbma9
C13sus
Bb13sus
PLAY
mf
1.
Bb9sus
2.
Bb9sus
Db9(#11)
C9sus
Bb9sus
Abma9
Gb13sus
Fmi11
E13sus
Ebma13(#11)
MOLTO RIT.

Presenting the Hal Leonard JAZZ PLAY-ALONG® SERIES

For use with all B-flat, E-flat, Bass Clef and C instruments, the Jazz Play-Along® Series is the ultimate learning tool for all jazz musicians. With musician-friendly lead sheets, melody cues, and other split-track choices on the included CD, these first-of-a-kind packages help you master improvisation while playing some of the greatest tunes of all time. FOR STUDY, each tune includes a split track with: melody cue with proper style and inflection • professional rhythm tracks • choruses for soloing • removable bass part • removable piano part. FOR PERFORMANCE, each tune also has: an additional full stereo accompaniment track (no melody) • additional choruses for soloing.

1. DUKE ELLINGTON
00841644 ..... $16.95

1A. MAIDEN VOYAGE/ALL BLUES
00843158 ..... $15.99

2. MILES DAVIS
00841645 ..... $16.95

3. THE BLUES
00841646 ..... $16.99

4. JAZZ BALLADS
00841691 ..... $16.99

5. BEST OF BEBOP
00841689 ..... $16.99

6. JAZZ CLASSICS WITH EASY CHANGES
00841690 ..... $16.99

7. ESSENTIAL JAZZ STANDARDS
00843000 ..... $16.99

8. ANTONIO CARLOS JOBIM AND THE ART OF THE BOSSA NOVA
00843001 ..... $16.95

9. DIZZY GILLESPIE
00843002 ..... $16.99

10. DISNEY CLASSICS
00843003 ..... $16.99

11. RODGERS AND HART FAVORITES
00843004 ..... $16.99

12. ESSENTIAL JAZZ CLASSICS
00843005 ..... $16.99

13. JOHN COLTRANE
00843006 ..... $16.95

14. IRVING BERLIN
00843007 ..... $15.99

15. RODGERS & HAMMERSTEIN
00843008 ..... $15.99

16. COLE PORTER
00843009 ..... $15.95

17. COUNT BASIE
00843010 ..... $16.95

18. HAROLD ARLEN
00843011 ..... $15.95

19. COOL JAZZ
00843012 ..... $15.95

20. CHRISTMAS CAROLS
00843080 ..... $14.95

21. RODGERS AND HART CLASSICS
00843014 ..... $14.95

22. WAYNE SHORTER
00843015 ..... $16.95

23. LATIN JAZZ
00843016 ..... $16.95

24. EARLY JAZZ STANDARDS
00843017 ..... $14.95

25. CHRISTMAS JAZZ
00843018 ..... $16.95

26. CHARLIE PARKER
00843019 ..... $16.95

27. GREAT JAZZ STANDARDS
00843020 ..... $15.99

28. BIG BAND ERA
00843021 ..... $15.99

29. LENNON AND MCCARTNEY
00843022 ..... $16.95

30. BLUES' BEST
00843023 ..... $15.99

31. JAZZ IN THREE
00843024 ..... $15.99

32. BEST OF SWING
00843025 ..... $15.99

33. SONNY ROLLINS
00843029 ..... $15.95

34. ALL TIME STANDARDS
00843030 ..... $15.99

35. BLUESY JAZZ
00843031 ..... $15.99

36. HORACE SILVER
00843032 ..... $16.99

37. BILL EVANS
00843033 ..... $16.95

38. YULETIDE JAZZ
00843034 ..... $16.95

39. "ALL THE THINGS YOU ARE" & MORE JEROME KERN SONGS
00843035 ..... $15.99

40. BOSSA NOVA
00843036 ..... $15.99

41. CLASSIC DUKE ELLINGTON
00843037 ..... $16.99

42. GERRY MULLIGAN FAVORITES
00843038 ..... $16.99

43. GERRY MULLIGAN CLASSICS
00843039 ..... $16.95

44. OLIVER NELSON
00843040 ..... $16.95

45. JAZZ AT THE MOVIES
00843041 ..... $15.99

46. BROADWAY JAZZ STANDARDS
00843042 ..... $15.99

47. CLASSIC JAZZ BALLADS
00843043 ..... $15.99

48. BEBOP CLASSICS
00843044 ..... $16.99

49. MILES DAVIS STANDARDS
00843045 ..... $16.95

50. GREAT JAZZ CLASSICS
00843046 ..... $15.99

51. UP-TEMPO JAZZ
00843047 ..... $15.99

52. STEVIE WONDER
00843048 ..... $15.95

53. RHYTHM CHANGES
00843049 ..... $15.99

54. "MOONLIGHT IN VERMONT" AND OTHER GREAT STANDARDS
00843050 ..... $15.99

55. BENNY GOLSON
00843052 ..... $15.95

56. "GEORGIA ON MY MIND" & OTHER SONGS BY HOAGY CARMICHAEL
00843056 ..... $15.99

57. VINCE GUARALDI
00843057 ..... $16.99

58. MORE LENNON AND MCCARTNEY
00843059 ..... $15.99

59. SOUL JAZZ
00843060 ..... $15.99

60. DEXTER GORDON
00843061 ..... $15.95

61. MONGO SANTAMARIA
00843062 ..... $15.95

62. JAZZ-ROCK FUSION
00843063 ..... $14.95

63. CLASSICAL JAZZ
00843064 ..... $14.95

64. TV TUNES
00843065 ..... $14.95

65. SMOOTH JAZZ
00843066 ..... $16.99

66. A CHARLIE BROWN CHRISTMAS
00843067 ..... $16.99

67. CHICK COREA
00843068 ..... $15.95

68. CHARLES MINGUS
00843069 ..... $16.95

69. CLASSIC JAZZ
00843071 ..... $15.99

70. THE DOORS
00843072 ..... $14.95

71. COLE PORTER CLASSICS
00843073 ..... $14.95

72. CLASSIC JAZZ BALLADS
00843074 ..... $15.99

73. JAZZ/BLUES
00843075 ..... $14.95

74. BEST JAZZ CLASSICS
00843076 ..... $15.99

75. PAUL DESMOND
00843077 ..... $14.95

76. BROADWAY JAZZ BALLADS
00843078 ..... $15.99

77. JAZZ ON BROADWAY
00843079 ..... $15.99

78. STEELY DAN
00843070 ..... $14.99

79. MILES DAVIS CLASSICS
00843081 ..... $15.99

80. JIMI HENDRIX
00843083 ..... $15.99

81. FRANK SINATRA – CLASSICS
00843084 ..... $15.99

82. FRANK SINATRA – STANDARDS
00843085 ..... $15.99

83. ANDREW LLOYD WEBBER
00843104 ..... $14.95

84. BOSSA NOVA CLASSICS
00843105 ..... $14.95

85. MOTOWN HITS
00843109 ..... $14.95

86. BENNY GOODMAN
00843110 ..... $14.95

87. DIXIELAND
00843111 ..... $14.95

88. DUKE ELLINGTON FAVORITES
00843112 ..... $14.95

89. IRVING BERLIN FAVORITES
00843113 ..... $14.95

90. THELONIOUS MONK CLASSICS
00841262 ..... $16.99

91. THELONIOUS MONK FAVORITES
00841263 ..... $16.99

92. LEONARD BERNSTEIN
00450134 ..... $15.99

93. DISNEY FAVORITES
00843142 ..... $14.99

94. RAY
00843143 ..... $14.99

95. JAZZ AT THE LOUNGE
00843144 ..... $14.99

96. LATIN JAZZ STANDARDS
00843145 ..... $14.99

97. MAYBE I'M AMAZED
00843148 ..... $15.99

98. DAVE FRISHBERG
00843149 ..... $15.99

99. SWINGING STANDARDS
00843150 ..... $14.99

100. LOUIS ARMSTRONG
00740423 ..... $15.99

101. BUD POWELL
00843152 ..... $14.99

102. JAZZ POP
00843153 ..... $14.99

103. ON GREEN DOLPHIN STREET & OTHER JAZZ CLASSICS
00843154 ..... $14.99

104. ELTON JOHN
00843155 ..... $14.99

105. SOULFUL JAZZ
00843151 ..... $15.99

106. SLO' JAZZ
00843117 ..... $14.99

107. MOTOWN CLASSICS
00843116 ..... $14.99

108. JAZZ WALTZ
00843159 ..... $15.99

109. OSCAR PETERSON
00843160 ..... $15.99

110. JUST STANDARDS
00843161 ..... $15.99

111. COOL CHRISTMAS
00843162 ..... $15.99

114. MODERN JAZZ QUARTET FAVORITES
00843163 ..... $15.99

115. THE SOUND OF MUSIC
00843164 ..... $15.99

116. JACO PASTORIUS
00843165 ..... $15.99

117. ANTONIO CARLOS JOBIM – MORE HITS
00843166 ..... $15.99

118. BIG JAZZ STANDARDS COLLECTION
00843167 ..... $27.50

119. JELLY ROLL MORTON
00843168 ..... $15.99

120. J.S. BACH
00843169 ..... $15.99

121. DJANGO REINHARDT
00843170 ..... $15.99

122. PAUL SIMON
00843182 ..... $16.99

123. BACHARACH & DAVID
00843185 ..... $15.99

124. JAZZ-ROCK HORN HITS
00843186 ..... $15.99

126. COUNT BASIE CLASSICS
00843157 ..... $15.99

Prices, contents, and availability subject to change without notice.

FOR MORE INFORMATION, SEE YOUR LOCAL MUSIC DEALER, OR WRITE TO:

HAL•LEONARD®
CORPORATION
7777 W. BLUEMOUND RD. P.O. BOX 13819
MILWAUKEE, WISCONSIN 53213

For complete songlists and more, visit Hal Leonard online at
www.halleonard.com

0910

Jazz Instruction & Improvisation

Books for All Instruments from Hal Leonard

AN APPROACH TO JAZZ IMPROVISATION

INCLUDES TAB

by Dave Pozzi

Musicians Institute Press

Explore the styles of Charlie Parker, Sonny Rollins, Bud Powell and others with this comprehensive guide to jazz improvisation. Covers: scale choices • chord analysis • phrasing • melodies • harmonic progressions • more.

00695135 Book/CD Pack $17.95

BUILDING A JAZZ VOCABULARY

By Mike Steinel

A valuable resource for learning the basics of jazz from Mike Steinel of the University of North Texas. It covers: the basics of jazz • how to build effective solos • a comprehensive practice routine • and a jazz vocabulary of the masters.

00849911 .....$19.95

THE CYCLE OF FIFTHS

by Emile and Laura De Cosmo

This essential instruction book provides more than 450 exercises, including hundreds of melodic and rhythmic ideas. The book is designed to help improvisors master the cycle of fifths, one of the primary progressions in music. Guaranteed to refine technique, enhance improvisational fluency, and improve sight-reading!

00311114 .....$16.99

THE DIATONIC CYCLE

by Emile and Laura De Cosmo

Renowned jazz educators Emile and Laura De Cosmo provide more than 300 exercises to help improvisors tackle one of music's most common progressions: the diatonic cycle. This book is guaranteed to refine technique, enhance improvisational fluency, and improve sight-reading!

00311115 .....$16.95

EAR TRAINING

by Keith Wyatt,

Carl Schroeder and Joe Elliott

Musicians Institute Press

Covers: basic pitch matching • singing major and minor scales • identifying intervals • transcribing melodies and rhythm • identifying chords and progressions • seventh chords and the blues • modal interchange, chromaticism, modulation • and more.

00695198 Book/2-CD Pack $24.95

EXERCISES AND ETUDES FOR THE JAZZ INSTRUMENTALIST

by J.J. Johnson

Designed as study material and playable by any instrument, these pieces run the gamut of the jazz experience, featuring common and uncommon time signatures and keys, and styles from ballads to funk. They are progressively graded so that both beginners and professionals will be challenged by the demands of this wonderful music.

00842018 Bass Clef Edition $16.95

00842042 Treble Clef Edition $16.95

JAZZOLOGY

THE ENCYCLOPEDIA OF JAZZ THEORY FOR ALL MUSICIANS

by Robert Rawlins and Nor Eddine Bahha

This comprehensive resource covers a variety of jazz topics, for beginners and pros of any instrument. The book serves as an encyclopedia for reference, a thorough methodology for the student, and a workbook for the classroom.

00311167 .....$18.95

JAZZ JAM SESSION

15 TRACKS INCLUDING RHYTHM CHANGES, BLUES, BOSSA, BALLADS & MORE

by Ed Friedland

Bring your local jazz jam session home! These essential jazz rhythm grooves feature a professional rhythm section and are perfect for guitar, harmonica, keyboard, saxophone and trumpet players to hone their soloing skills. The feels, tempos and keys have been varied to broaden your jazz experience. Styles include: ballads, bebop, blues, bossa nova, cool jazz, and more, with improv guidelines for each track.

_____00311827 Book/CD Pack $19.99

JAZZ THEORY RESOURCES

by Bert Ligon

Houston Publishing, Inc.

This is a jazz theory text in two volumes. **Volume 1 includes:** review of basic theory • rhythm in jazz performance • triadic generalization • diatonic harmonic progressions and analysis • substitutions and turnarounds • and more. **Volume 2 includes:** modes and modal frameworks • quartal harmony • extended tertian structures and triadic superimposition • pentatonic applications • coloring "outside" the lines and beyond • and more.

00030458 Volume 1 .....$39.95

00030459 Volume 2 .....$29.95

Prices, contents & availability subject to change without notice.

JOY OF IMPROV

by Dave Frank and John Amaral

This book/CD course on improvisation for all instruments and all styles will help players develop monster musical skills! **Book One** imparts a solid basis in technique, rhythm, chord theory, ear training and improv concepts. **Book Two** explores more advanced chord voicings, chord arranging techniques and more challenging blues and melodic lines. The CD can be used as a listening and play-along tool.

00220005 Book 1 – Book/CD Pack $27.99

00220006 Book 2 – Book/CD Pack $24.95

THE PATH TO JAZZ IMPROVISATION

by Emile and Laura De Cosmo

This fascinating jazz instruction book offers an innovative, scholarly approach to the art of improvisation. It includes in-depth analysis and lessons about: cycle of fifths • diatonic cycle • overtone series • pentatonic scale • harmonic and melodic minor scale • polytonal order of keys • blues and bebop scales • modes • and more.

00310904 .....$14.95

THE SOURCE

THE DICTIONARY OF CONTEMPORARY AND TRADITIONAL SCALES

by Steve Barta

This book serves as an informative guide for people who are looking for good, solid information regarding scales, chords, and how they work together. It provides right and left hand fingerings for scales, chords, and complete inversions. Includes over 20 different scales, each written in all 12 keys.

00240885 .....$15.95

21 BEBOP EXERCISES

by Steve Rawlins

This book/CD pack is both a warm-up collection and a manual for bebop phrasing. Its tasty and sophisticated exercises will help you develop your proficiency with jazz interpretation. It concentrates on practice in all twelve keys – moving higher by half-step – to help develop dexterity and range. The companion CD includes all of the exercises in 12 keys.

00315341 Book/CD Pack $17.95

FOR MORE INFORMATION, SEE YOUR LOCAL MUSIC DEALER, OR WRITE TO:

7777 W. BLUEMOUND RD. P.O. BOX 13819 MILWAUKEE, WI 53213

Visit Hal Leonard online at **www.halleonard.com**

0910

ARTIST TRANSCRIPTIONS®

Artist Transcriptions are authentic, note-for-note transcriptions of today's hottest artists in jazz, pop and rock. These outstanding, accurate arrangements are in an easy-to-read format which includes all essential lines. Artist Transcriptions can be used to perform, sequence or for reference.

CLARINET

00672423 Buddy De Franco Collection $19.95

FLUTE

00672379 Eric Dolphy Collection $19.95
00672372 James Moody Collection – Sax and Flute.....$19.95
00660108 James Newton – Improvising Flute $14.95

GUITAR & BASS

00660113 The Guitar Style of George Benson.....$14.95
00699072 Guitar Book of Pierre Bensusan $29.95
00672331 Ron Carter – Acoustic Bass.....$16.95
00672307 Stanley Clarke Collection.....$19.95
00660115 Al Di Meola – Friday Night in San Francisco $14.95
00604043 Al Di Meola – Music, Words, Pictures.....$14.95
00673245 Jazz Style of Tal Farlow $19.95
00672359 Bela Fleck and the Flecktones.....$18.95
00699389 Jim Hall – Jazz Guitar Environments $19.95
00699306 Jim Hall – Exploring Jazz Guitar $19.95
00604049 Allan Holdsworth – Reaching for the Uncommon Chord $14.95
00699215 Leo Kottke – Eight Songs.....$14.95
00675536 Wes Montgomery – Guitar Transcriptions $17.95
00672353 Joe Pass Collection $18.95
00673216 John Patitucci.....$16.95
00027083 Django Reinhardt Antholog $14.95
00026711 Genius of Django Reinhardt.....$10.95
00672374 Johnny Smith Guitar Solos $16.95
00672320 Mark Whitfield $19.95

PIANO & KEYBOARD

00672338 Monty Alexander Collection $19.95
00672487 Monty Alexander Plays Standards.....$19.95
00672318 Kenny Barron Collection $22.95
00672520 Count Basie Collection.....$19.95
00672364 Warren Bernhardt Collection $19.95
00672439 Cyrus Chestnut Collection $19.95
00673242 Billy Childs Collection.....$19.95
00672300 Chick Corea – Paint the World.....$12.95
00672537 Bill Evans at Town Hall.....$16.95
00672425 Bill Evans – Piano Interpretations $19.95
00672365 Bill Evans – Piano Standards.....$19.95
00672510 Bill Evans Trio – Vol. 1: 1959-1961 .....$24.95
00672511 Bill Evans Trio – Vol. 2: 1962-1965 .....$24.95
00672512 Bill Evans Trio – Vol. 3: 1968-1974 .....$24.95
00672513 Bill Evans Trio – Vol. 4: 1979-1980 .....$24.95
00672381 Tommy Flanagan Collection.....$24.99
00672492 Benny Goodman Collection $16.95
00672486 Vince Guaraldi Collection.....$19.95
00672419 Herbie Hancock Collection.....$19.95
00672438 Hampton Hawes $19.95
00672322 Ahmad Jamal Collection $22.95
00672564 Best of Jeff Lorber $17.99
00672476 Brad Mehldau Collection $19.99
00672388 Best of Thelonious Monk $19.95
00672389 Thelonious Monk Collection.....$19.95
00672390 Thelonious Monk Plays Jazz Standards – Volume 1 .....$19.95
00672391 Thelonious Monk Plays Jazz Standards – Volume 2 .....$19.95
00672433 Jelly Roll Morton – The Piano Rolls.....$12.95
00672553 Charlie Parker for Piano.....$19.95
00672542 Oscar Peterson – Jazz Piano Solos.....$16.95
00672544 Oscar Peterson – Originals $9.95
00672532 Oscar Peterson – Plays Broadway.....$19.95
00672531 Oscar Peterson – Plays Duke Ellington $19.95
00672563 Oscar Peterson – A Royal Wedding Suite $19.99
00672533 Oscar Peterson – Trios.....$24.95
00672543 Oscar Peterson Trio – Canadiana Suite $9.95
00672534 Very Best of Oscar Peterson $22.95
00672371 Bud Powell Classics.....$19.95
00672376 Bud Powell Collection $19.95
00672437 André Previn Collection $19.95
00672507 Gonzalo Rubalcaba Collection.....$19.95
00672303 Horace Silver Collection.....$19.95
00672316 Art Tatum Collection.....$22.95
00672355 Art Tatum Solo Book $19.95
00672357 Billy Taylor Collection $24.95
00673215 McCoy Tyner $16.95
00672321 Cedar Walton Collection $19.95
00672519 Kenny Werner Collection $19.95
00672434 Teddy Wilson Collection.....$19.95

SAXOPHONE

00672566 The Mindi Abair Collection.....$14.99
00673244 Julian "Cannonball" Adderley Collection $19.95
00673237 Michael Brecker $19.95
00672429 Michael Brecker Collection $19.95
00672315 Benny Carter Plays Standards.....$22.95
00672314 Benny Carter Collection.....$22.95
00672394 James Carter Collection $19.95
00672349 John Coltrane Plays Giant Steps $19.95
00672529 John Coltrane – Giant Steps $14.95
00672494 John Coltrane – A Love Supreme $14.95
00672493 John Coltrane Plays "Coltrane Changes" $19.95
00672453 John Coltrane Plays Standards $19.95
00673233 John Coltrane Solos.....$22.95
00672328 Paul Desmond Collection.....$19.95
00672379 Eric Dolphy Collection $19.95
00672530 Kenny Garrett Collection $19.95
00699375 Stan Getz.....$19.95
00672377 Stan Getz – Bossa Novas $19.95
00672375 Stan Getz – Standards.....$18.95
00673254 Great Tenor Sax Solos.....$18.95
00672523 Coleman Hawkins Collection $19.95
00673252 Joe Henderson – Selections from "Lush Life" & "So Near So Far".....$19.95
00672330 Best of Joe Henderson $22.95
00673239 Best of Kenny G.....$19.95
00673229 Kenny G – Breathless.....$19.95
00672462 Kenny G – Classics in the Key of G $19.95
00672485 Kenny G – Faith: A Holiday Album.....$14.95
00672373 Kenny G – The Moment $19.95
00672326 Joe Lovano Collection $19.95
00672498 Jackie McLean Collection $19.95
00672372 James Moody Collection – Sax and Flute.....$19.95
00672416 Frank Morgan Collection $19.95
00672539 Gerry Mulligan Collection.....$19.95
00672352 Charlie Parker Collection $19.95
00672561 Best of Sonny Rollins.....$19.95
00672444 Sonny Rollins Collection $19.95
00675000 David Sanborn Collection $17.95
00672528 Bud Shank Collection.....$19.95
00672491 New Best of Wayne Shorter.....$19.95
00672550 The Sonny Stitt Collection $19.95
00672350 Tenor Saxophone Standards $18.95
00672567 The Best of Kim Waters.....$17.99
00672524 Lester Young Collection $19.95

TROMBONE

00672332 J.J. Johnson Collection $19.95
00672489 Steve Turré Collection $19.95

TRUMPET

00672557 Herb Alpert Collection $14.99
00672480 Louis Armstrong Collection $17.95
00672481 Louis Armstrong Plays Standards $17.95
00672435 Chet Baker Collection $19.95
00672556 Best of Chris Botti $19.95
00672448 Miles Davis – Originals, Vol. 1 .....$19.95
00672451 Miles Davis – Originals, Vol. 2 .....$19.95
00672450 Miles Davis – Standards, Vol. 1 .....$19.95
00672449 Miles Davis – Standards, Vol. 2 .....$19.95
00672479 Dizzy Gillespie Collection $19.95
00673214 Freddie Hubbard $14.95
00672382 Tom Harrell – Jazz Trumpet $19.95
00672363 Jazz Trumpet Solos $9.95
00672506 Chuck Mangione Collection $19.95
00672525 Arturo Sandoval – Trumpet Evolution....$19.95

FOR MORE INFORMATION, SEE YOUR LOCAL MUSIC DEALER, OR WRITE TO:

HAL•LEONARD® CORPORATION

7777 W. BLUEMOUND RD. P.O. BOX 13819 MILWAUKEE, WI 53213

Visit our web site for a complete listing of our titles with songlists at
www.halleonard.com

Prices and availability subject to change without notice.

The Best-Selling Jazz Book of All Time Is Now Legal!

The Real Books are the most popular jazz books of all time. Since the 1970s, musicians have trusted these volumes to get them through every gig, night after night. The problem is that the books were illegally produced and distributed, without any regard to copyright law, or royalties paid to the composers who created these musical masterpieces.

Hal Leonard is very proud to present the first legitimate and legal editions of these books ever produced. You won't even notice the difference, other than all the notorious errors being fixed: the covers and typeface look the same, the song lists are nearly identical, and the price for our edition is even cheaper than the originals!

Every conscientious musician will appreciate that these books are now produced accurately and ethically, benefitting the songwriters that we owe for some of the greatest tunes of all time!

VOLUME 1
Includes: Autumn Leaves • Body and Soul • Don't Get Around Much Anymore • Falling in Love with Love • Have You Met Miss Jones? • Lullaby of Birdland • Misty • Satin Doll • Stella by Starlight • and hundreds more!

00240221 C Edition $29.99
00240224 B♭ Edition $29.95
00240225 E♭ Edition $29.95
00240226 Bass Clef Edition $29.95
00240292 C Edition 6 x 9 ..... $27.95
00451087 C Edition on CD-ROM $25.00

VOLUME 2
Includes: Avalon • Birdland • Come Rain or Come Shine • Fever • Georgia on My Mind • It Might as Well Be Spring • Moonglow • The Nearness of You • On the Sunny Side of the Street • Route 66 • Sentimental Journey • Smoke Gets in Your Eyes • Tangerine • Yardbird Suite • and more!

00240222 C Edition $29.95
00240227 B♭ Edition $29.95
00240228 E♭ Edition $29.95
00240229 Bass Clef Edition $29.95
00240293 C Edition 6 x 9 ..... $27.95

VOLUME 3
Includes: Ain't Misbehavin' • Cheek to Cheek • The Lady Is a Tramp • A Nightingale Sang in Berkeley Square • On a Clear Day • Stormy Weather • The Very Thought of You • and more!

00240233 C Edition $29.99
00240284 B♭ Edition $29.95
00240285 E♭ Edition $29.95
00240286 Bass Clef Edition $29.95

Also available:

THE REAL VOCAL BOOK
00240230 Volume 1 High Voice $29.95
00240307 Volume 1 Low Voice $29.99
00240231 Volume 2 High Voice $29.95
00240308 Volume 2 Low Voice $29.95

THE REAL BOOK – STAFF PAPER
00240327 ..... $9.95

NOW AVAILABLE: Play-along CDs to some of the most popular songs featured in the world famous *Real Books*. Each volume features selections sorted alphabetically from the 6th edition.

The Real Book Play-Along – Volume 1 A-D
00240302 3-CD Set $24.95

The Real Book Play-Along – Volume 1 E-J
00240303 3-CD Set $24.95

The Real Book Play-Along – Volume 1 L-R
00240304 3-CD Set $24.95

The Real Book Play-Along – Volume 1 S-Z
00240305 3-CD Set $24.95

The Real Book Play-Along – Volume 2 A-D
00240351 3-CD Set $24.99

The Real Book Play-Along – Volume 2 E-I
00240352 3-CD Set $24.99

The Real Book Play-Along – Volume 2 J-R
00240353 3-CD Set $24.99

The Real Book Play-Along – Volume 2 S-Z
00240354 3-CD Set $24.99

For More Information, See Your Local Music Dealer, Or Write To:

7777 W. Bluemound Rd. P.O. Box 13819 Milwaukee, WI 53213

Complete song lists online at www.halleonard.com

Prices and availability subject to change without notice.

0210